Hyaena

Hyaena   Hans Kruuk

OXFORD UNIVERSITY PRESS 1975

Oxford University Press, Ely House, London W.1

GLASGOW NEW YORK TORONTO MELBOURNE WELLINGTON
CAPE TOWN IBADAN NAIROBI DAR ES SALAAM LUSAKA
ADDIS ABABA DELHI BOMBAY CALCUTTA MADRAS KARACHI
LAHORE DACCA KUALA LUMPUR SINGAPORE HONG KONG
TOKYO

ISBN 0 19 857379 0

Filmset and printed in Great Britain by BAS Printers Limited, Wallop, Hampshire

Contents

Our hunting grounds

With all our modern knowledge of biology, and with all our ability in large-scale data handling, we are still a long, long way from evaluating all the variables in the life of an animal in its own environment. I do not regret this lack of information, because it allows us 'curious naturalists' to wander about and justify our existence, marvelling at fascinating new observations, wondering about their biological implications and adaptive significance. Some day, perhaps, all such field observations will be slotted into a large, exact matrix, into a proper systems analysis. But happily that day is still far away.

One only has to follow a large animal around for a few days in order to recognize the complexity of its relationship with its environment and other animals; there is much more to it than modern ecology and ethology are yet able to express. Somehow these disciplines are still unable to study and describe the whole animal, and the things that make it tick. This is probably one of the reasons why I felt dissatisfied after writing down the results of my study of spotted hyaenas in a book about the species' ecology and behaviour. Too many naturalists' titbits had to be left out, pictures and details which seemed to have little significance for the understanding of predator–prey relations or of social organization, but which somehow are important if one tries to get an idea of the whole animal in its whole environment, which shaped its behaviour during evolution. I hope that the following pages will give a vivid impression of the actual life of the hyaena, of its excitement and languor, its hunger and satiation.

2. Pyjama-lily, *Crinum kirkii*

3. Genet, foraging

1. Serengeti plains, with wildebeest and zebra

4. Dwarf mongoose on look-out post

7

1. Python swallowing Egyptian goose

Spotted hyaenas, or 'Fisi' (their Swahili name), in their hunting and in their social organization, show several characteristics which they appear to share with primitive man. Maybe it is this which makes them especially interesting to follow in their exploits and contacts; perhaps it is easier to imagine the world through their eyes than through those of a rabbit, or a bear, or a bird. I studied them and part of their environment, the Serengeti and Ngorongoro, in East Africa.

Serengeti means 'open grassland plains' in the Masai language. There is much more in this area than just open grassland, yet the name aptly describes its main characteristic. About half of the 10,000 square mile area which we now call Serengeti is National Park, famous for its huge, migrating herds of wildebeest and gazelle, for its lions and leopards, and for its tremendous space. It lies just east of Lake Victoria, in Tanzania.

8

3. Hippo

The Ngorongoro Crater, immediately southeast of the Serengeti, is only 100 square miles. Still it looks huge; a large bowl bubbling with wild-life. Its grasslands, marshes, and lake are completely surrounded by the steep crater wall, and with more or less the same animals living there as in the Serengeti it is almost a choice sample of the latter.

For seven years, my wife Jane and I lived in the centre of the Serengeti National Park, most of the time in a wooden prefabricated bungalow. Animals were around us everywhere: large herds made the walls vibrate sometimes, buffalo came and scraped their backs against the corner of the house, hyaenas frequented the verandah at night, lion, cheetah, and wild dog came almost within touching distance, and we saw almost 200 different species of birds from the house. One could be really perfectly happy to sit on that verandah for ever, with a pair of field glasses and maybe a drink. Now, afterwards, I sometimes regret that we didn't sit and enjoy the views from the house more often; such a great deal of time was spent 'on safari', camping in the Park or in the Ngorongoro.

The house always had a lot of visitors—other scientists or their wives who also worked in the area, park wardens, tourists, or old friends. Especially the contacts with the park wardens were essential to us; their difficulties with running the park, their struggle with poachers, and even their criticisms of our scientific efforts were a constant reminder of what we were there for—to help in conservation, to provide background knowledge for the management of these beautiful areas.

4. Tourism in the Crater

5. Masai rock drawing (recent): shield, man, and lion

2. Crowned cranes over drinking zebra

Every year tens of thousands of tourists and naturalists come to see these places, but they are not able to spend longer than a day or so; they usually miss the early mornings and the moonlit nights, which are really the times to see things happen. In fact, no visit there is long enough; the longer one stays the more one experiences the fantastic richness and variety. Something new and unexpected is always happening, even after you have been there many years. This is not surprising in a place like the Serengeti, where there are well over 50 large mammal species, including 27 carnivores, not to mention the many small mammals, over 400 birds, many insects, and a rich vegetation.

The Serengeti and Ngorongoro offer a fantastic opportunity to study the relationships between animals and environment, an opportunity which has been taken up successfully by the Serengeti Research Institute. However, the studies of most of its scientists (including my own) have been largely involved with ecological problems—these are of prime importance to *conservation* of the area. But I could not help being fascinated even more by other aspects of our work, by the intricate adaptations of animal behaviour, which really strike one everywhere in these wonderful areas.

1. Elephant

3. Marabou storks feeding in the flooded crater lake (note dead acacia trees)

4. Fighting warthog males

These adaptations might be found in the way in which a snake eats a bird, or a warthog uses its knobbly face in a fight, or a genet searches for insects between the rocks—each gesture is significant to survival, indicating something of the role of this behaviour and this animal in its world. And whilst gazing at this profusion of interwoven detail I was struck forcibly by something which many ecologists overlook: many important relationships between species only express themselves in the beautifully adapted reactions to each other and their environment. For example, a predator may not eat a certain prey simply because the quarry is always successful in eluding it, and there are many other examples. Ecologically speaking such relationships are not very interesting—but in order to understand the evolution of living systems a behaviourist will want to know about them.

Perhaps the best way to begin to understand the confusing variety of animal life in places like the Serengeti and Ngorongoro is to concentrate one's attention on one species, rather than to try and study many simultaneously. Thus in this short story of the spotted hyaena, I hope that the reader will appreciate something of the way in which all aspects of hyaena biology hang together—hunting and social behaviour, defaecation and territory, sex and dominance—and all this in apparent harmony with the ever changing environment. In the process, one might also catch a glimpse of the life of many other animals which feature in the hyaena's surroundings.

Whenever, in the following pages, I refer to 'hyaenas' (or to 'fisi') I shall mean the spotted hyaena, *Crocuta crocuta* Erxleben. Other members of the family will be mentioned in the last section of the book. All photographs were taken in Serengeti or Ngorongoro, except where stated otherwise.

Foraging
Activity

The most depressing aspect of hyaenas' behaviour from their admirers' point of view is their tendency to sleep for hours and hours, sometimes even days. In fact, more than four-fifths of their time is spent lying down. Having said that, I must add that they do a good deal in the remaining time to make up for this; but usually their behaviour is shrouded in darkness, and they certainly don't make it easy for a human observer to watch it. Most of the hyaenas' activity takes place during the first half of the night; then there is a clear break after midnight, followed by further exertions in the last couple of hours before daybreak.

Watching them at night is difficult; hyaenas move far and fast, across gullies and marshes where cars often cannot follow. Modern night-viewing instruments such as infrared and electronic image-intensifier devices still cannot quite cope with these problems; they are too cumbersome, with a small field and restricted range. Radio transmitters on the animals help a great deal—but for straightforward watching one still needs the bright African moonlight on the days near full moon, a very good knowledge of the area, and a good pair of binoculars. Fortunately, hyaenas sometimes show some of their more interesting behaviour in daylight, especially in the short time before sunrise.

1, 2, 3, 4. Hyaenas in daytime

5, 6. Grooming before getting active

During the day hyaenas lie up in all sorts of cool places—rarely in their den, but often in warthog holes, under trees or shrubs, just somewhere on the grass, and especially near water or in the mud. They love mud, sometimes lying in it up to their necks; if disturbed, they will only pull themselves out of it with great reluctance to the accompaniment of gorgeous mud-sucking noises.

7. Yearling having a drink

Scavenging and hunting

Everybody knows that hyaenas are scavengers. This is true enough; one should only add that the same can be said for most other carnivores —they prefer an easy meal to one which they have to catch first. Hyaenas scavenge where they can, but usually there isn't that much to pick up, and then they kill. This means that in both Ngorongoro and Serengeti the majority of hyaena food was killed by the animals themselves; Serengeti hyaenas scavenged a bit more than their Ngorongoro colleagues because there were more dead animals available.

Why then have hyaenas, more than other carnivores, acquired their particular reputation? Probably it is because when man sees 'fisi' it is usually in the animal's capacity as a scavenger—around a hunter's camp at night, on a kill with vultures by day. Furthermore, the spotted hyaenas' striped relative comes in contact with civilization much more often, in India, the Middle East, North Africa—and that species is much more of a scavenger than the spotted. Another reason for the hyaenas' bad name lies in the misinterpretation of their relationship with lions.

Scavenging is usually a rather solitary business for hyaenas; they walk around through the bush and over the plains, picking up a bone here and there, and spending hours or even days around a carcass, or an African village. Their physiology, their musculature, and particularly their teeth are very well adapted to making use of almost every ounce on a kill, every scrap of skin, and every splinter of bone.

Watching hyaenas dismember a carcass gives a good indication of just how effective they are in this. But this effectiveness applies to the way in which they deal with their own kills just as much as to their manner of consuming left-overs from others.

1. Scavenging around a wild dog kill, with golden jackal. Note the wildebeest's curiosity

Fig. 3.

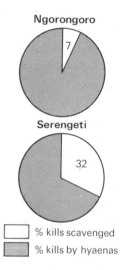

Ngorongoro

7

Serengeti

32

☐ % kills scavenged

▨ % kills by hyaenas

2. Licking her lips near a kill

4. Pack hunting at night

1. Solitary foraging

Once, after a wild zebra chase by 25 hyaenas, I saw two zebras, a mare and her one year-old foal, disappear absolutely and completely into the ravenous mouths of the pack—in a period of less than 40 minutes. That was the first time that I had come across the incredible speed of hyaenas' eating, but since then I have noticed it time and again. A heavy wildebeest carcass, for instance, some 400 lbs, may vanish in much less than an hour once the pack of hyaenas starts work on it; there may be some hyaenas left here and there chewing a bone or the head —but after a few hours those parts also will have disappeared down the ever hungry gullets. Only the horns and the teeth are not eaten; hair is later regurgitated or passed with the faeces, but everything else is digested. The horns will go too, eventually, eaten by moths—only they take somewhat longer over it.

The main characteristics of hyaenas which make this extraordinarily fast and efficient process possible are their teeth and their digestive physiology. Incisors and canines are used for pulling off chunks of soft meat, and the real hard work is done by three bone-crushing pre-molars on each side of the mouth, and by the carnassial sheer right in the back, which deals with tough skin and tendons. The three blunt bone-crushers can deal even with large buffalo leg bones, noisily splintering them before they are swallowed.

1. Aggression over a wildebeest leg
3. Hyaena skull

2. Injuries from hyaena bites. This wildebeest bull was killed by a lion (throat bite) after it had been grabbed and mauled by hyaenas

4. The bone-crunching mechanism

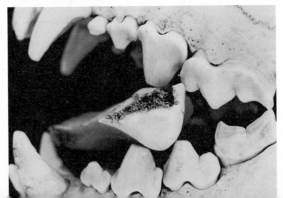

5. The last part to go of the carcass: stripping down the hea

6. Cutting skin with carnassial shear

8. All that remains of a wildebeest bull: the horns, a few splinters of bone, some regurgitated hair, and white hyaena faeces

In the stomach the bone is completely digested; the faeces consist of a very fine powder, of the same chemical composition as bone, but without all its collagen. Since bone may contain over one-third of this particular protein the bone-chewing habit of hyaenas must be a very worthwhile habit. This is the explanation for the animal's strangely white droppings —although Masai have it that the colour comes from the hyaenas eating ashes of their fires!

9. Even the horns soon disappear, eaten by the larvae of the moth *Tinea deperdella*. The protuberances are cocoons

7. Pulling off soft parts with incisors

Competition over a carcass

Not only can hyaenas eat very fast, but they are also able to swallow huge quantities. I found, for instance, that an animal would be able to eat well over 30 lbs, one third of its own body weight, in one meal—although its average daily need is somewhere in the order of 5–7 lbs. Of course, some parts of the carcass are preferred to others; all this means that

1–5. Feeding competition in Ngorongoro—every scrap is used

there is bound to be competition over food, even at a large carcass, as soon as hyaenas gather. The larger the number, the hotter the competition. Hyaena density is different in the various areas I worked in, and clearly the Ngorongoro hyaenas have to compete with many more colleagues than those in Serengeti. Whatever the ecological implications of this are, it is interesting to see how the species' behaviour is adapted to deal with this scramble for food: each animal wolfs down as much as it can, as quickly as possible, then tears off a large chunk, leg or head, and withdraws from the madding crowd to eat in some safe place.

There is remarkably little fighting amongst members of a group, but a great deal of noisy calling.

In the Serengeti such scrambles are less common, and there one frequently finds the carcass of an animal which died of starvation or disease without any hyaena ever having been near it. This would never happen in the Ngorongoro Crater, where there are so many more hyaenas to each living herbivore. The huge migrations of the grass eaters in the Serengeti make it impossible for carnivores, at least for young ones, to keep up, so there are relatively fewer hyaenas and lions. In Ngorongoro they have increased to the level of fierce competition amongst themselves.

6. Mean number of hyaenas eating a carcass of:

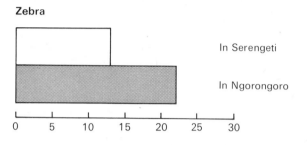

Wildebeest

In Serengeti

In Ngorongoro

Zebra

In Serengeti

In Ngorongoro

0   5   10   15   20   25   30

7, 8. Food abundance in the Serengeti

One early morning, after a dark night with heavy winds and rain, I found 82 gazelle lying dead, 27 badly injured, all fairly close

together near the edge of the Serengeti plains. A few of them had been partly eaten, and tracks showed that hyaenas were responsible for this massacre. I had seen this sort of thing before, with foxes in an English gull colony, and here again, I was struck by the apparent waste of it all. Probably such cases are natural accidents, where the normally well-adapted behaviour of the animals breaks down in the face of very unusual circumstances. Hyaenas, like other carnivores, do not always kill for food—even when they are not hungry they will seize an easy opportunity to grab an animal, then store the carcass or leave it for relatives to eat. During the very heavy storm of that particular night the gazelle had been lying down, unable to see and run, and hyaenas could quietly walk from one to the next, killing or stunning, then walk on. Their behaviour is programmed to deal with some superabundance of food but, in the face of such fantastic food surplus, all was left to the vultures.

1–4. Thomson's gazelle, victims of a massacre by hyaenas (in right hand picture a sample of them collected for dissection)

5. Searching for the cache

Many carnivores have their own methods of storing food: leopards drag it up a tree, jackals and foxes bury it in the ground, striped

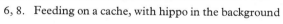
6, 8. Feeding on a cache, with hippo in the background

7. Gazelle remains stored by hyaenas in shallow mudhole

hyaenas stick it in a bush. But I think spotted hyaenas are the most ingenious. They drop chunks of a kill into shallow water, usually deep enough to cover it completely, but only where there are no crocodiles. They are pretty good at retrieving it, too, plunging their heads deep under water in the approximate spot and searching around until they bump into it.

21

1. Searching for food: in packs, or solitary

Hunting

Wildebeest, zebra, gazelle—these animals are the regular food for hyaenas, usually caught after a wild and exciting hunt. Watching hyaenas chase the prey of their choice at night is an immensely impressive experience; there is the sudden action, the wild run, the gasps of the victim. Afterwards one remembers the deep black silence over it all, surrounding the rush of a hundred hooves. Then the kill, steaming in the chill air, with a hyaena cacophony over and around it.

Perhaps this hunting for food was the aspect of hyaena behaviour which surprised people most when they were told about it. But the story becomes even more interesting once one looks at the details of this hunting, for one begins to notice that zebras are hunted differently from wildebeest, and gazelle differently again; hyaenas have a typical way of dealing with each of their many food species. Some prey is hunted by a hyaena on its own, for some species the hunter is joined by more hyaenas at the end of the chase, whilst for others again hyaenas form large packs long before they have even contacted the potential victim. In the following pages I want to demonstrate some of these differences, and show that these variations on a hunting theme are not just useless frills—they make up a beautifully functional arrangement to deal with the often very effective anti-predator mechanisms of the quarry. It is the contrast between the group and the individual, between social and solitary existence, which indicates these intricate adaptations that deal with the pressures of existence.

1. Searching for fawns around a mixed herd of Grant's (foreground) and Thomson's gazelle

2. Thomson's gazelle fawn, crouching

3. Herd of Thomson's gazelle, mostly females

4-7. Chasing a 'stotting' Thomson's gazelle male

Quietly, seemingly uninterested in its surroundings, a solitary hyaena walks past a herd of Thomson's gazelle (tommies), as if it were going somewhere far away. The little gazelle fawn would have been all right, lying well concealed in the grass just off the hyaena's path—but it jumped, ran, bleated, until the hyaena's jaws closed around its shoulders some hundred yards further on.

Fawns are the most common category of gazelle-food for hyaenas, but frequently adult tommies or granties are also chased and taken. Which is rather strange, for gazelle on the whole are so much faster than hyaenas. But once a predator has disturbed animals in a herd, and begins to chase an individual gazelle, the quarry gives the impression that it is not really exerting itself; it stays just in front of the pursuer, at speeds of perhaps 30–40 m.p.h. At the beginning of the chase the tommie 'stots' along, bounding off the ground on all four legs simultaneously, providing a most striking display to all the gazelle around; probably, this functions as an alarm signal. Once the hyaena gets close, however, the tommie changes into a faster, flat-out run—with the hyaena doggedly on its heels. This may go over two or three miles, and often the hyaena gives up, but one in five of the chased gazelle slows, and finds the hyaena getting closer and closer. Then the quarry performs some spectacular sharp cornering before the hyaena grabs, disembowels, dismembers, and digests it. One or two other hyaenas may join in the feasting; essentially, however, the gazelle hunt is a one-hyaena affair.

25

Hunting wildebeest

In several ways the hunt for wildebeest is similar to that for gazelle; there is the fast, long-distance run of a single hunter behind a lonely quarry on the open, grassy plains. But in at least two ways wildebeest hunting is strikingly different. First, in the manner in which an animal is selected. A hyaena stands and watches wildebeest filing past on their way to or from a grazing area; the wildebeest hardly show whether they have noticed the attentive predator some yards away. Or the hyaena itself will walk slowly in the moonlit crater night, close to a black herd, from which emerge occasional grunts. Suddenly then there is silence from the herd; action—the hyaena speeds along into the wildebeest crowd, scattering them in front, letting them close ranks again behind. Some fast running, zigzagging with the tail streaming behind, and the hyaena stops again, looking at the running animals, perhaps in the way in which a horse dealer studies the trot of a potential buy. This is the time when the hyaena might decide on a particular individual and start running again, flat out now, perhaps after a bull who now speeds across the plain, out of the herd, quite on his own. Still only one hyaena is involved (at least in three-quarters of my observations), looking minute behind the big black wildebeest. The chase may last a couple of hundred yards, or it may be three miles, and while watching it the second difference with the tommie-hunt becomes clear: more hyaenas join in, and when, finally, the bull turns to face his tormentors he finds jaws everywhere. If this point is reached no wilde-

1. Wildebeest herd at nightfall

3. Alarmed bull running off ▷

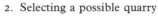

2. Selecting a possible quarry

1. Hunting a bull at night: confrontation at the end of the chase

2. Grabbing the quarry

3. Collapse

4. Eating

beest ever escapes; the quarry hardly defends himself, swaying his horns somewhat uselessly, moaning at the incessant merciless bites. When the hungry hordes have pulled him down there may be as many as 52 hyaenas feeding from the carcass.

Not all the wildebeest which are chased are killed of course. The hyaenas' success rate was about one in three; in the other, unsuccessful chases the wildebeest often escaped by outrunning the 'fisi', or, less frequently, by disappearing into the anonymity of another herd of wildebeest or by reaching the hyaenas' territorial boundary with their neighbours. Many times the plagued animal would head for water, a little river or a lake—but on those occasions it was invariably bagged by the hyaenas. I have no idea what the function is of this inclination to take the plunge—wildebeest are hopeless performers in water. This is a question which perhaps will be solved some day by another study, looking at wildebeest in a quite different situation.

5. Bull seeking refuge in water

6, 7. Kill in the river

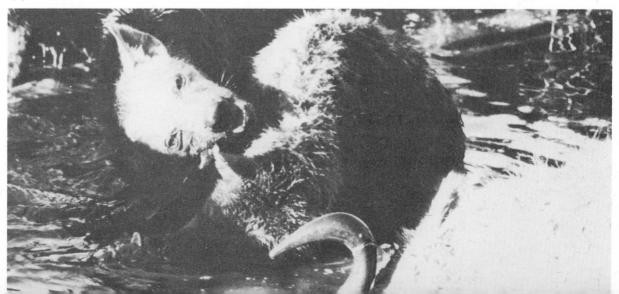

Hunting wildebeest calves

1. Calves with their mothers

2. Fast run of a single hunter

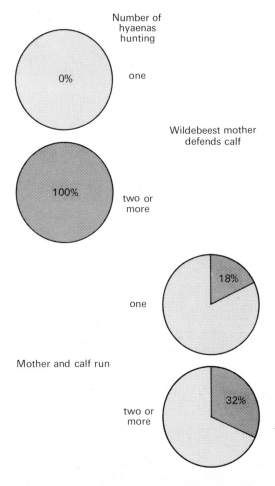

3. After the kill

Number of hyaenas hunting

0%   one

Wildebeest mother defends calf

100%   two or more

Mother and calf run

one   18%

two or more   32%

4. Percentage successful hunting attempts (shaded) by on or more hyaenas hunting wildebeest calves

In the course of a few weeks in January and February every wildebeest cow produces a calf. It is a beautifully timed, synchronous operation; quite suddenly there are these masses of small beige animals running through the black herds, sticking very close to their mothers. These calves are very vulnerable; if they lose their mothers they will die, they are conspicuous, and they are very easy meat for carnivores during their first days of life. But the calving areas are simply swamped with a superabundance of easy prey, and predators just cannot eat them all that quickly; this must be one of the main functions of the striking synchronization of births. Hyaenas gorge themselves on wildebeest calves during this short time of the year, and they appear to have an uncanny ability for recognizing calves which will give them an easy run, that is, the very young ones. Calves can run fast within about an hour after being born, but not fast enough to shake off a 'fisi'; even when they are a day old, a hyaena is able to catch up within a few hundred yards. Then all depends on what the wildebeest cow does, and how many hyaenas there are; I found that in this game a hyaena on its own is five times less successful than when accompanied by one or two others. It is easy to see the reason for this difference; if the cow defends her offspring with her horns (she doesn't always), one hyaena can go round the back and grab the calf while the other keeps the mother busy. It is a beautiful demonstration of increase in efficiency through cooperation between hunters.

Hunting flamingoes

At times there may be several hundred thousand lesser flamingoes on the little lake in the Crater, feeding in the soda water only a few inches deep. They come and go at night, reluctant to fly in daytime—unless somebody makes them. A few single hyaenas have taken to sorting them out, checking the presence of sick or injured birds. The way hyaenas do this is very reminiscent of how they select wildebeest from a herd—making them move by dashing into the crowd, watching for the animal that cannot keep up with its mates, then running after it, splashing through the shallows. But this flamingo craze has never really caught on amongst the hyaenas; there are only few individuals who indulge in flamingo hunting, mostly two- or three-year-olds who would always come last when a carcass is to be shared with other, older hyaenas. The beautiful flamingoes are probably only inferior food to hyaenas.

4, 5, 6, 7. Search, selection, and kill of a lesser flamingo

Hunting zebra

A few groups of zebra were standing on the grass plains close to the lake in the Ngorongoro Crater, just before the last light was to fade from the sky. They were family groups, and I was looking at one in particular, a stallion with five mares and three foals, which was getting a bit restless. The animals' heads were up, and all were staring at a pack of 14

hyaenas walking towards them in a slow, steady, almost purposeful way. The hyaenas stopped 10 yards away, and both parties just stood and looked; then slowly the stallion, his head low, walked out from his family towards the hyaenas. He put on some speed, and in no time the hyaenas turned and scattered out of his way; the end of another typical, and frequent, interaction between the two species.

The hyaenas approached the next zebra family in a similar fashion; again the stallion attacked, but this time the hyaenas just avoided him without losing interest in his family.

The mares and foals bunched up and began to walk away slowly; the hyaena pack followed menacingly, spread out in a crescent behind the zebra. Suddenly the scene was full of action: the stallion attacking individual hyaenas and attempting to bite, to kick with his fore-legs; excited barking from one of the mares; hyaenas running everywhere, avoiding the stallion, aiming at the now running zebra family. One hyaena grabbed a mare in the loins and lost his grip; the chase continued, Then another mare was grabbed, slowing down only slightly; within seconds she was

1. Zebra family

standing alone in a seething crowd of hyaenas, her family disappearing, her stallion abandoning the defence. She just stood, silent; the only sound came from hyaena jaws working on her skin, while far away now the other zebras kept on their high-pitched, excited barking; cranes called from the lake. An hour later there was nothing left to mark the spot, except a large, dark patch on the grass. Later I found the mare's jaw, and I could determine her age from the teeth; she had been an apparently healthy, middle-aged animal, approximately 10 years old.

2. Pack, ready for action

This was a typical zebra hunt; overall, about one-third of the zebra chases as described here end in the death of one of the hunted. But note the enormous difference between this and the way in which, for instance, a wildebeest is chased; hyaenas invariably attack zebra in a pack of up to 25 participants (average 11), which has formed usually long before the zebra is contacted. When one follows such a group, it is clear that the hyaenas are much less interested in other prey species; they may walk a long distance through wildebeest herds to get to the nearest zebra families. There is

no doubt in my mind that pack hunting is adopted by hyaenas to deal with the vicious attacks of the zebra stallion in defence of his family—a single hyaena just wouldn't have a chance against that. And a zebra as prey seems to provide a reward well worth the social effort—an individual hyaena gets much more from a zebra kill than from, for instance, a wildebeest carcass.

Zebra hunt at night: confrontation, chase, pulling down, and kill

Hunting rhino

The rhinoceros, that huge, armoured animal weighing up to 3000 lbs, can hardly be expected to be a fair prey for hyaenas. They are left in peace, though sometimes a party of boisterous 'fisi' may spend some time 'rhino-baiting'—it looks just like a game. But one evening I saw a mother rhino with a small calf walking past a hyaena den, just as it was getting dark, when suddenly hyaenas converged on the pair from all directions. About 25 hyaenas attempted to grab the calf, whilst its mother and the calf itself put up a very spectacular resistance. At the end of a 2½ hour fight the calf had lost its ears and its tail, and was bleeding from many wounds—but the two were still holding out.

Then unexpectedly another hyaena came running past on the heels of a wildebeest bull, and given the choice the attacking hyaenas chose to follow up the wildebeest rather than the rhino calf. The wildebeest was killed, and the rhino calf survived; two weeks later I met it again, looking rather shapeless without its normal appendages, but otherwise perfect. The calf was saved more or less by accident, but I have no doubt that on other occasions the hyaenas' combined efforts against the rhino's defence would be successful. The observation certainly indicated why some adult rhinos are earless!

1. Black rhinoceros with buff-backed heron: an impenetrable fortress

4. Masai—morani (warrior)

2, 3. Rhinos in Ngorongoro Crater, speared by Masai, eaten by hyaenas after they died in agony with spears in their body

Adult rhinos may land up in the hyaenas' stomachs, often through interference by man. In Ngorongoro many rhinoceroses are being speared by Masai boys, apparently just for the sport of it, and the authorities are unable to do very much about it. The rhinos die a slow death on the crater floor, with spears sticking out of their body—easy meat for the carnivores and vultures. If the present rate of rhino mortality continues these enormous chunks of aggression will be a very rare sight in the Ngorongoro Crater a few years from now.

5, 6, 7. Attempt to kill a rhino calf at night

1. The zebra family, a small, closely protected unit

2. Eland; adults defend the herd

3. The

Adaptation of hunting

Hyaenas catch different kinds of animals with different strategies, involving single hyaenas only, or packs of them, or something in between. What is more, it seems that the hunters 'decide' before even contacting the prey which species they are going to chase. I can recognize, for instance, a pack of zebra hunters even if there are no zebra nearby, and I know that they will catch up with them later. Why this differentiation: what is the function of it all?

Perhaps it is not difficult to understand the small numbers of hyaenas involved in the capture of a gazelle or of a flamingo: the reward is only small, and each prey animal acts for itself only; there is no communal defence. The comparison of attacks on wildebeest and zebra is more interesting; there I think that the wildebeest selection would be difficult to carry out with a group of hyaenas and might result in absolute chaos, whilst at the final capture of a wildebeest some assistance by other hyaenas comes in very useful.

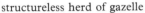
structureless herd of gazelle

4. Communal defence of the formidable buffalo

As far as zebras are concerned, a single hyaena just wouldn't have a hope against the teeth and hooves of an aggressive stallion who defends his family group. The same would also be true in a confrontation with a rhinoceros. It is interesting that animals such as eland and buffalo are hardly ever taken on by hyaenas, except when they are on their own. Not only are they large and prepared to use their horns, but their very tight social organization in which members actually defend each other and each other's calves (unlike the wildebeest) makes hyaena predation virtually impossible. Twice I saw an eland calf almost taken when it ventured out on its own, but in both cases it reached the herd in time and the hyaenas were faced with a wall of horns, just as in the classical case of musk ox defending themselves against wolves.

Much of this goes to demonstrate the adaptedness of the hyaena's hunting behaviour; it also indicates the need for a very flexible social system which can provide solitary hunters one moment, and a pack in the next. It is somewhat ironic to think that the species with this complicated behaviour organization was supposed to be a mere scavenger!

39

5. A Serengeti herd of wildebeest: each one fends for itself

Competition

Once the attention of biologists was focused on the 'struggle for survival' it became evident that competition is a dominant aspect in the lives of many animals. Everywhere one sees competition for food, for chances to reproduce, for protection against various sources of mortality. But it sometimes seems as if spotted hyaenas receive more than their fair share of environmental pressures, for not only does every individual have other hyaenas against it, but each meal is contested by a variety of creatures ranging from vultures and crocodiles to all the other large carnivores, and man. In the following pages I want to show something of the various odds against which a hyaena has to contend, and the way in which it turns some of this carnivorous competition to its advantage.

2. Wild dogs retrieving stolen property

Wild dogs before the hunt

Competition: wild dogs

Fourteen wild dogs streamed over the vast open grasslands, in a flat-out run after a single Thomson's gazelle. The tommy cornered sharply when the first dog came close, and the pursuer overshot widely, losing considerable ground. But the second dog in the sequence was there to cut the corner, closing in on the gazelle only to overshoot equally badly after another sharp turn by the tommy. Then the quarry ran into the third dog, who grabbed it. All the dogs descended in a cloud of dust on the fallen victim, eating silently, with only the occasional whimpering of an aggressive younger dog amongst them.

Gazelle are the dogs' usual prey in the Serengeti (67 per cent of my 115 observations), followed by wildebeest calves (17 per cent); they are killed after a long chase, usually by daylight. Thus, the dogs' main interest in the herbivores is somewhat different from that of spotted hyaenas—but the latter often come in to scavenge a piece after the wild dogs have killed, and that is where their interests overlap most. At three in four of the wild dog kills in the Serengeti, hyaenas were there to either chase off the dogs, or just steal a piece, or to eat some left-overs. In return, I saw only five occasions where wild dogs chased off hyaenas from a kill which could be called hyaena property. So in this case, hyaenas derive almost all the benefits of the association, but by no means without difficulty. Although hyaenas are heavier and stronger, wild dogs will often combine to attack a hyaena, never killing (to my knowledge) but sometimes drawing blood. The treatment they mete out would be sufficient deterrent to most animals perhaps—except to 'fisi'. But hyaenas don't

41

1. Hyaena stealing remains of a topi-calf

2. Wild dogs just after grabbing a topi-calf

3. Hyaena slinking around a wild dog kill (tommy fawn)

always get their own way; the outcome of a clash between dogs and hyaenas must be to some extent determined by the numbers of each, their hunger, and previous experience. From the hyaenas' point of view, as well as our own, it is a great pity that wild dogs are not more common—probably those in Serengeti and Ngorongoro combined amount to fewer than 300. The species is still being shot in the bordering game reserves which is no good augury for their future.

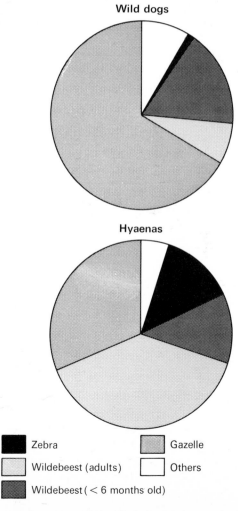

Wild dogs

Hyaenas

■ Zebra   Gazelle

☐ Wildebeest (adults)   ☐ Others

▨ Wildebeest (< 6 months old)

43

4. Comparison of the diet of wild dogs and hyaenas, in the Serengeti

1. Running towards a hyaena kill

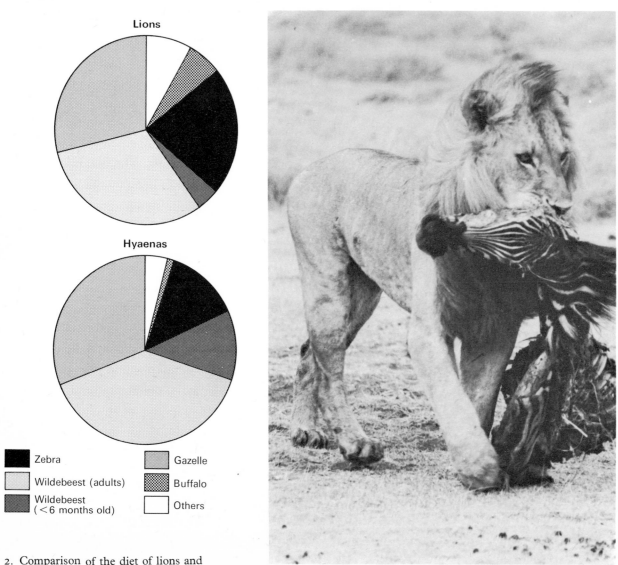

Lions

Hyaenas

■ Zebra

▨ Gazelle

▢ Wildebeest (adults)

▦ Buffalo

▨ Wildebeest (<6 months old)

▢ Others

2. Comparison of the diet of lions and hyaenas in the Serengeti

3. Walking off with a stolen carcass

Competition: lions

Few African carnivores have so many interests in prey species in common as the lion and the spotted hyaena. Consequently, the two are continually at loggerheads. This is not just a one-way process of hyaenas following lions to steal some food remains, as popular belief has it; if anything it is the other way round, at least in some areas. When watching my hyaenas in the Ngorongoro Crater after they had made a kill, it was quite common to suddenly hear one of the feasting hunters utter the soft, staccato alarm grunt at which all heads would go up, staring in one direction. It might be a false alarm, but more often than not one would see the King of Beasts trotting up from a distance, in an ungainly hurry. Usually the lion went straight for the carcass left by the hyaenas who scattered in all directions, but sometimes he first gave the 'fisi' a good chase, though rarely actually catching and killing one. I just could not help muttering nasty things about lions when one turned up at a hyaena kill, because usually this meant the end of the action for a long time: the lion

44

4. Hyaenas attempting to retrieve their kill from a lioness

5. Lioness catching old hyaena female

6. Killed by a lion when the latter raided a hyaena kill

settled down to eat, and might be at the kill for hours and hours, sometimes even days, with hyaenas keeping in the background. Here I found one of the reasons for the hyaenas' bad reputation; when they eat their own kill, it takes them very little time to make a carcass disappear completely, but they may stay for many hours around a lion who has stolen their kill. And because lions eat slowly, with long pauses, the casual daylight visitor will often find the large cats on a carcass with hyaenas hanging around, and will draw the obvious but wrong conclusion that hyaenas are waiting for the spoils from the lion kill. Rarely does a tourist find hyaenas eating their own kill, and little does he know of their nocturnal goings on!

The Ngorongoro lions with their huge black manes must be amongst the most beautiful in the world. They seem to thrive in their particular way of life, but to the hyaenas there they must be a pest. During my studies from 1964 to 1968 lions stole one in five of the hyaena kills in the Crater, but during a six week visit in 1972 this figure had increased to three in four. The extent to which lions scavenge from hyaenas (or vice versa) probably depends on the absolute and relative numbers of carnivores present in the area. In the Ngorongoro Crater there is a dense population of hyaenas and there are so many for each lion present that it is possible for a lion to live almost entirely by scavenging from them rather than kill for himself. But in the Serengeti things are different, lions have to kill more for themselves, thus giving hyaenas a better chance to collect some food from lion kills. This taking of food by the hyaenas is by no means confined to merely lapping up the spoils after the cats have left; hyaenas are quite capable of 'shifting' a lion from a kill with some not-too-gentle persuasion. Here, as in the interactions with wild dogs, their hunger and previous experience seems to determine the outcome of a clash over food.

Having watched so many tussles over kills, on arriving to find both hyaenas and lions there, I now have a fair idea how to judge who was the killer of the carcass. Usually lions lie next to the corpse, hyaenas keeping well out of harm's way; if in such a situation a leg or tail is missing I know that the 'fisi' were there before the lions as the latter do not carry large

45

1. Hyaenas on wildebeest kill. Alarm: lion approaching   2, 3. Chasing off the owners

pieces away, or at least not far (they may carry the whole carcass to a sheltered place). A bloody-mouthed hyaena may give the game away, and one can compare the amount eaten from the carcass with the size of the lions' stomachs. I check up on the temperature of the kill (it gives a clue about the length of time

46

6, 7, 8, 9. Lions on hyaena kill at night, surrounded by the hunters and blackbacked jackals, and defending their new-found property

4. Lion with the carcass

5. Hyaenas returning after lion's withdrawal

it has been dead), and check on bites in the throat or around the nostrils and on scratches along the side of the body (lion kill), or on bites in abdomen and hind legs (hyaena kill). After all this one still cannot always be sure, and then the observation goes into the 'doubtful' category (which is embarrassingly large).

47

Mostly because of these fights over kills, lions are the major cause of mortality amongst adult hyaenas in these areas. The big cats hardly ever eat a victim of their wrath, however; sometimes a lion tears the hyaena carcass apart, then leaves it. But if a lion falls under hyaena teeth, its killers have no hesitation about turning the enemy into good food, and several times I found lion hair and claws in hyaena regurgitations or droppings.

To a birdwatcher who has seen song birds mob an owl it is interesting to watch hyaenas do almost exactly the same thing to a lion: they walk closely behind or around a lion who may be merely passing by, they whoop, giggle, and low at it, but scatter when the lion only so much as looks at them. Yet, this mobbing may have the effect of pushing the lion a little bit further out of the way than he would otherwise have been. Occasionally this mobbing may turn into less inhibited aggression: several times I watched lions being attacked at night by a crowd of hyaenas, the lion escaping up a tree or into a dense bush, sometimes bleeding. But this kind of clash is relatively rare, and more often it is the hyaena who gets the worst of an encounter with a lion.

1. Drinking at night, whilst keeping an open ear for the sound of hyaenas on a kill

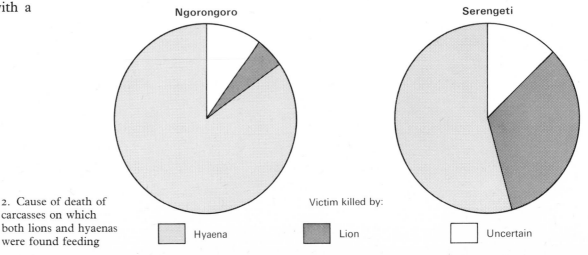

2. Cause of death of carcasses on which both lions and hyaenas were found feeding

Ngorongoro

Serengeti

Victim killed by:

Hyaena   Lion   Uncertain

48

Competition: man

Whilst I was looking at the contents of some hyaena droppings which I had found on the border of the Serengeti National Park, I quite unexpectedly found some short curly black hairs between those of wildebeest and zebra—remains of a person, probably Masai. This was the first proof I had of 'fisi's' anthropovorous habits, and since then my evidence of their nuisance value to man has been piling up. Around human settlements hyaenas may eat livestock; they may take animals from poachers' snares; they may attack children or people asleep in the open. So they can be a profound nuisance, but man gets a little in return for all this. For instance, hyaenas dispose of human corpses which many tribes in East Africa still put out in the bush for this purpose, and in the Ethiopian town of Harar hyaenas are the principal dustmen. On the other hand few people ever have the opportunity to appreciate a tommy steak scavanged from a hyaena kill as I did, and it is true to say that in general the relation between hyaena and man is very one-sided. To natives and visitors of Africa alike, no creatures are more

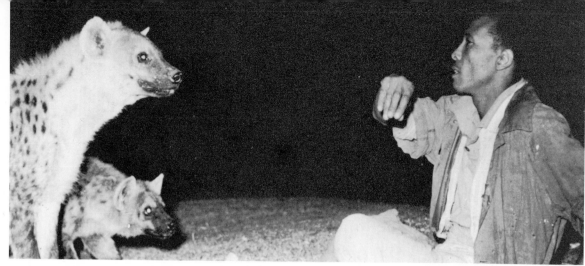

3. Hyaenas on almost, but not quite, friendly terms with people in Harar, Ethiopia

loathsome than 'fisi'. Even the South African Bushmen, who relish eating brown hyaenas, will not touch the meat of the spotted species.

This loathing goes beyond feelings based on mere ecological competition; it may well be that a primitive fear is involved, arising from the knowledge that hyaenas are 'the living mausoleum of the dead', as someone described them. Aren't the animal's weird laughing noises and its slinking nocturnal movements around one's house (often followed by some disaster to the occupants) almost proof that

in some devilish way it is under the control of supernatural powers? I, too, must admit to a shiver along my spine when once, in the rain at midnight, I was out with a torch looking along a swollen river in the Serengeti for a man we feared drowned. I met a silent, very quiet hyaena who walked past me without much notice. The man we searched for was found the next day, dead, close to the place where I had stood.

Undoubtedly, hyaenas play a more important role in African witchcraft than any other

4. Hyaena remains: the poison-arrow tells the story

5. Ghostly appearance at night

animal, and in this continent witchcraft is very commonly practised. People known to be witches ride hyaenas at night (that is why hyaenas's backs are sloping), laughing madly, while casting their spells on other people. Not only do witches ride hyaenas, they also keep them at home, and they live off hyaena-milk and hyaena-butter, and use this butter to fuel their torches. According to some villagers one can smell for days the places where witches spilled burned butter from their torches (the smell of the hyaenas' territorial scentmarking). Luckily, one can protect oneself and one's cattle against the evil influence of witches by feeding the animals ground-up pieces of dried hyaena skin, genitals, or heart, or smearing those substances into small cuts in one's arm. But no one should kill a 'fisi' for otherwise the witch-owner is bound to take revenge. All this may sound weird, perhaps childish, to a non-African reader. But the beliefs are real, nevertheless, very real, and common. It was only in 1971 that a hyaena was killed in the centre of the town of Musoma, on Lake Victoria; in a matter of hours the corpse had disappeared, divided up in very small pieces by the townspeople, to be used as charms.

In complete contrast to this strange, deep fear which the Africans display towards the hyaena is the role which the latter plays in the many animal stories that African mothers tell their children. There he is the butt of the tale, the stupid, greedy, loutish beast that always ends up either being beaten, or tortured, or killed. His role is somewhat like that of Bruin the bear, in old European stories.

1. Scavenging around the townships (Harar, Ethiopia)

GIRL MAULED BY HYENA IS SAVED AFTER MERCY FLIGHT

By NATION Reporter

A BRAVE young Boran girl lay in a Nairobi hospital bed yesterday recovering from her ordeal after being savagely mauled by a marauding hyena.

The girl, Godano Wario, 12, was attacked by the hyena while asleep in a hut at Merti in the Isiolo area in the early hours of yesterday morning.

2. Some recent newspaper cuttings from East Africa

Hyenas kill patient

A 70-year-old patient in Shinyanga hospital was killed by hyenas on Friday night when he was leaving the hospital without permission. He was admitted to the hospital for bronchial complaints.

The hospital staff rushed to rescue him but they found him already dead.

Hungry hyenas grab cyclist

Three hungry hyenas chased a schoolmaster Nyirendas Luggage, as he was cycling to work, flung him from his bicycle and badly mauled him before villagers answered his cries for help.

The Malawi Newsagency reported the incident which happened in the Nkata Bay district on Lake Malawi. The hyenas were tracked down by a game ranger who shot two of them dead and wounded the third.

Hyenas attack Homa Bay cemetery—report

By NATION Correspondent

A NUMBER of graves in the Homa Bay cemetery are understood to have been attacked by hyenas and a number of bodies eaten in recent days.

A correspondent there quoting Mzee Omol Achuku, commonly known as "Mayor", said the number of hyenas visiting the lake-shore town, especially during the night, had increased considerably in recent days.

It is understood that the hyenas live on a small hill near the town. At night they invade the town searching for food.

Residents of the town have requested the authorities concerned to deal with the menace as soon as possible.

After all this it comes perhaps as a surprise that hyaenas make such very nice pets—somewhat rough and boisterous, but very affectionate and intelligent, in general character somewhat between a cat and a dog. Our Solomon was found by rangers in the extreme west of the Serengeti, sitting in front of a den. After we had picked him up he used our house as his den, free to come and go as he pleased, and often we took him out for long walks in the Park. At first Jane gave him milk from a bottle, but later we had to still his voracious appetite by bringing back parts of kills, which we had found in the bush. He was a marvellous and fascinating companion, and if he had not become so hooked on cheese in the bar of the tourist lodge, and bacon off the Chief Park Warden's breakfast table, he would still be with us; he had little difficulty opening doors anywhere. Unfortunately, not everybody was as fond of hyaenas as we were, and Solomon was banned from the National Park to spend the rest of his days in Edinburgh Zoo.

4. Jane and Solomon for a walk in the Crater

3. Masai woman

Competition: jackals

The largest game habitually hunted by jackals is gazelle, both Grant's and Thomson's, and mostly very young animals at that. They are very successful in this, especially when members of a pair combine forces; jackals on their own are mostly chased away by the mother gazelle. Because of this defence by the mother, a pair of jackals will successfully catch a gazelle fawn in four attempts out of six, but a jackal on its own has only one-quarter of this success rate. In fact, most of the jackal's food consists of insects, small rodents and fruits, and they are inveterate scavengers. They dart in and out of the turmoil around a carcass, between the legs of

1. Golden jackal defending its kill against Rüppell's griffon

2, 3, 4. Blackbacked jackal pair catching fawn of Thomson's gazelle: while one chases the mother, the other catches the fawn, and they eat it together

the larger carnivores, slinking off with little morsels in their mouths which they then often hide somewhere; or they steal food from vultures. In areas like the Ngorongoro they often obtain a large amount of food from hyaena kills, but every so often hyaenas steal a jackal's tommy fawn; benefit is mutual, though perhaps the jackal gets the better deal.

There are three species of jackal in Serengeti and Ngorongoro, with remarkably similar habits. These three, the golden, the black-backed, and the stripe-sided jackal do show some interesting differences, but generally the similarities are much more striking than the differences between them.

I have often seen a hyaena accidentally walk close to the den of a jackal; in those cases, he was left in no doubt about where he was. Invariably the jackal, of whichever species, ran up to the intruder, barked, and bit the hyaena's hindlegs. I have never seen a hyaena who seriously resisted this ignominious treatment—he always put his tail between his legs and lolloped off. Size is obviously not everything.

5. Whilst one eats the outside, the other cleans out the contents (golden jackal and hyaena on carcass of black rhino)

1. The descent of vultures marks a carcass

Competition: vultures

Vultures are the all-time scavengers of the African plains and bush; they will be there at the spoils of almost every kill; they may fly above a pack of wild dogs or hyaenas, landing when a wildebeest is grabbed. They will sit on the branch of a tree shading a zebra with a broken leg, and hundreds will drop out of the sky on a rhino dying with a spear in its flank. Vultures consume great quantities of meat in a very short time, and there is no doubt that without them many carnivores, especially hyaenas, would have much more food available.

Vultures may be a major competitive force, but as far as hyaenas are concerned, they have their uses. I first became fully aware of this when once, in the heat of mid-day, I sat drowsily watching a hyaena who was fast asleep in a mudhole. Four vultures came plummeting down on something half a mile away, out of sight beyond a rise. I could hear the wind through the feathers of the enormous diving birds, and so obviously could the hyaena; it jumped up, took one look at the distant black spots disappearing below its horizon, then spurted off, emerging a short

while later carrying part of a gazelle carcass. Such incidents soon turned out to be quite common, and they are probably an important cause for the hyaena's reputation as a scavenger. Over the years in the Serengeti I noted that hyaenas are much more likely to scavenge during the day (when tourists may be watching them) than at night. This difference can be explained almost entirely by the activities of vultures, which only fly by day.

54

Sometimes hyaenas are fooled by the birds, in a way which provides an interesting natural experiment to show that it is, indeed, the alighting vultures that draws the hyaenas, and not the carcass itself. At the beginning of the rainy season large flocks of white and Abdim's storks alight on the plains, on their migration south from Europe and North Africa. Then hyaenas come running up, looking around somewhat sheepishly amidst the storks before slowly walking back to their resting place. But it is only with the first flock of arriving storks that hyaenas are taken in this way; they soon learn to discriminate between storks and vultures, though it looks as if they have to learn this lesson again every year!

Although one often talks about vultures as if they belonged to only one species there are in fact six, all of them active in Ngorongoro and Serengeti in their own way, all of them competing with carnivores and each other

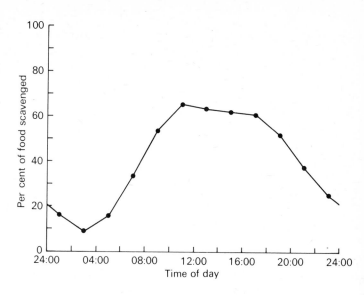

2. When hyaenas eat in daytime they are more likely to have scavenged their food than when they eat at night—an effect due largely to the activities of vultures

over almost every carcass. They are the white-backed vulture (who make up 64 per cent of the vulture population), the Rüppells griffon (13 per cent), the lappet-faced (12 per cent), the whiteheaded (3 per cent), the hooded (8 per cent), and the Egyptian vulture (1 per cent). Very rarely one sees the bearded vulture or lammergeyer, the specialist in breaking bones, but commonly there are tawny eagles, marabou storks, ravens, or kites amongst the vultures.

The whiteheaded vulture may be one of the less common species, but this is the one that often finds a carcass first, especially early in the morning. Then other species of vultures soon follow, after they have detected the carcass by seeing the discoverer land. It may

1. White-headed vulture

2. Hooded (left) and Egyptian vulture

3. Rüppell's griffon

4. White-backed vulture

5. Lappet-faced vulture

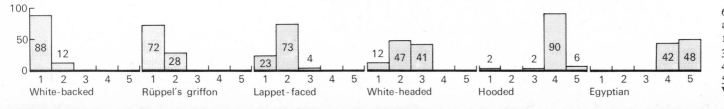

6. Different vultures eat different parts of a carcass: diet of the six Serengeti species.
1 = soft meat, 2 = skin and tendons, 3 = large pieces of meat around carcass, 4 = small pieces of meat around carcass, 5 = small bits from bones around carcass. Vertical is per cent of observations

be because they are better built for flapping flight than the other large species, which are typically high-level soaring birds, that white-headed vultures are particularly good at finding carcasses. The small vultures (hooded and Egyptian) arrive last, and these observations fit in neatly with what I saw of the feeding behaviour, for having arrived at the carcass in a certain order the vulture species then select different parts of it—although there is a considerable overlap of interest.

Lappet-faced vultures and Rüppell's griffons are much more aggressive than the rest, especially to their own species; if they do attack others, the ones that most often spark off their aggression are the species with which they share most interests in the carcass—in other words the species which are ecologically closest.

There are many other behaviour patterns in which the vultures differ from each other on the feeding grounds, and which contribute to their ecological separation. Their reactions to carnivores, for instance, vary a great deal: lappet-faced and whiteheaded vultures keep well away from lions or hyaenas, whilst hooded and Egyptian vultures feed amongst them, and the other two species are more or less intermediate.

7. Aggression between two Rüppell's griffons

8. Hyaenas and white-backed vultures in competition

57

1. White-backed vulture waiting for an opening

Therefore, although one may see six species of vulture feeding from one carcass in what at first seems a massive disorganized scramble, there is in fact considerable differentiation in the way in which they set about it. The two species which show more rivalry between them than any others are the whitebacked vulture and the Rüppell's griffon, as they have the same food interests and arrival times. The Rüppell's griffon is larger and more aggressive and it can chase off whitebacks without difficulty; but its numbers may well be restricted by something which has little to do with the competition for food. It is entirely dependent on large cliffs for nesting, and those are few and far between compared with the tall tree canopies selected by whitebacks for their nests. But in any case, the geographic area of overlap between the two species is small, and there are only a few places where they have to suffer each other to the same extent as in Serengeti and Ngorongoro.

The differentiation of feeding habits which evolved amongst vultures enables them to make use of vast quantities of carrion. From the hyaenas' point of view—what a waste!

2. Vultures on a rhino carcass: white-backs, and one lappet-faced vulture

Ostriches seem comparatively safe from predation. They are formidable runners, and although in the dry season the ostrich must be one of the most important vertebrates on the Serengeti plains hyaenas, at least, seem to ignore them almost completely. But all the same, these carnivores focus their attention on the ostrich's eggs and chicks. An ostrich sits on a massive assembly of eggs, products of several hens who each contribute 7–10 eggs to a cock's family; 30 eggs in a nest is not exceptional. Such a nest is usually well-guarded, but frequently one finds eggs lying alone, unattended on the open plain—real ostrich drop-outs; a hyaena finding such a treasure will spend considerable time in trying to reach the contents. This is no easy matter, and more often than not hyaenas give up after many attempts to get their jaws around the enormous smooth structure. But there's more than one road leading to Rome, and sometimes the carnivore is able to make use of the services provided by other animals, as is shown by this case history of one ostrich egg found in the Ngorongoro Crater.

1. Ostrich nest: the products of three hens

2. Ostrich hen: little fear of a hyaena

3, 4. A golden jackal finds an ostrich egg, licks and rolls it over 8 yards, then leaves it when two hyaenas approach

5, 6, 7. Hyaenas jostling whilst biting at the egg, then they leave it

8, 9, 10. An Egyptian vulture alights, walks off and returns with a stone, opens the egg and eats

11, 12, 13. The Egyptian vulture has hardly begun to eat before being displaced by two hooded vultures, who themselves wouldn't be able to open an ostrich egg

14, 15, 16, 17. The commotion attracted a hyaena, who walked off with the dripping egg, to eat it in a quiet spot

1. One earmarked male with his pack mates

Social behaviour

Clans and territories

Hyaenas scavenge and kill, they are driven off by lions, and they chase vultures. But what about the relations between hyaenas themselves? To get a better idea of this I had to know individuals, and I had to mark them. The technique I used was to drive the Land Rover as close as possible to an animal—this had to be within 100 ft—then fire a drug-laden syringe at it, from a dart-gun. The drug I used was succinyl-chlorine chloride, which caused paralysis; some five minutes after being hit the hyaena would collapse, and I was able to mark it by clipping triangles out of its ears. This made it recognizable even by moonlight, and over long distances. Twenty minutes later the animal would walk off again, none the worse for its experience—although perhaps its appearance had suffered somewhat.

2. Hit with a dart, but not quite immobilized yet

3. Removing the dart before earmarking

From the movements of these marked hyaenas a picture of their social organization could be drawn, which turned out to be fascinating. Fundamental to the hyaenas' society in Ngorongoro is their clan-system: the animals are organized in groups of between 30 and 80 hyaenas, and each of these 'clans' occupies a large area which is well-defined. The whole 100 square mile crater is divided up between eight clans. In Serengeti the system is somewhat more complicated because of the migratory habits of the animals there, but the underlying principles appeared the same.

Each clan has a central den, and it defends its range against its neighbours. Individual hyaenas know exactly where the boundaries are, and if they happen to be chasing a quarry across into their neighbours' area, they often give up the chase on the border.

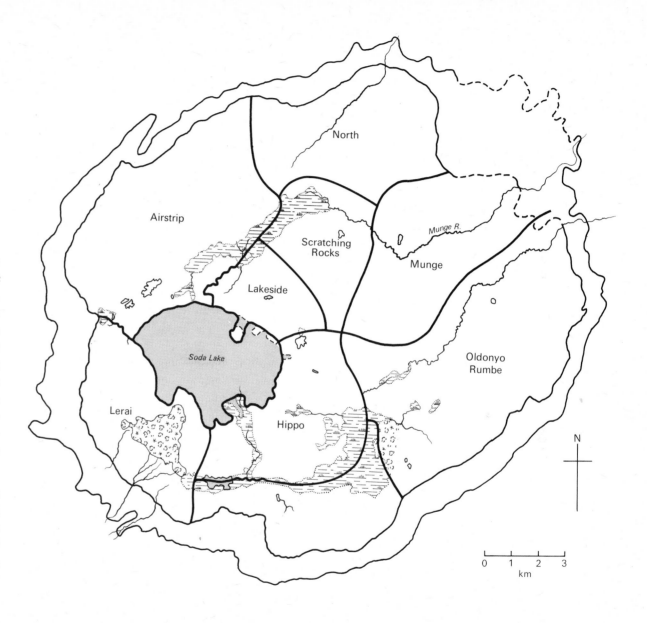

4. Results of the marking programme: the clan ranges of Ngorongoro

A single hyaena who crosses into its neighbouring clan lands may be severely punished, but the most spectacular defence of territory takes place when whole packs of hyaenas meet, usually over a kill. A wildebeest may be pulled down in the border region, or just across the boundary—then the neighbours will turn up in force. If they chase the trespassing hunters off their kill they are often chased away again themselves, and a carcass may change hands many times this way, with the 'armies' rushing backwards and forwards to the accompaniment of an unbelievable cacophony of sounds. If a single hyaena is caught by the enemies it is mauled, often killed, sometimes eaten later. I have seen as many as 70 hyaenas involved in such a clan clash, and especially at night such a little war is chaos only decipherable to a hyaena.

1, 2, 3, 4. Clash between two clans: a kill on the boundary which the neighbours try to steal, but the owners of the carcass see them off

Boundaries of clan territories are strongly defended—they are also clearly marked. Small parties of hyaenas regularly 'patrol' the borders; they walk along it and chase any hyaena who does not belong to their side. But the most important activity of these patrols seems to be marking the boundary: special marking sites are established all along it, which I simply called the 'lavatories'. When a party, usually 6–10 animals, arrives at such a place the hyaenas get quite excited, scratching the ground, and several of them will defaecate. Even I can clearly smell the secretion of interdigital glands in the scratch marks on the ground, and these lavatory sites must, to a hyaena, stand out very strikingly.

1. Marking the borders: a patrol busily 'pasting' and scratching the ground on a 'lavatory' (faeces in foreground)

2. Pasting

3. Defaecating

4. Scratching the ground

5. About to chase an intruder

The animals also leave a secretion of the anal glands pasted on grass stalks—the lavatory is usually sited in a patch of long grass. But this 'pasting' is done everywhere in the clan range, not just on the boundary, although there is quite a concentration of pasting there. The yellowish secretion, barely visible on the grass, smells strongly of something like cheap soap or rancid butter. It is interesting that even very young hyaenas perform this pasting around the den, although their anal glands don't work yet, so they have nothing to show for their efforts.

6. Lavatory

7. Pasting by a 2-month old: the behaviour is there, but the glands don't work yet

Dens

The centre of all clan activities is the den—often sited in flat grassland and consisting simply of a collection of holes; there may be just a few entrances, or two dozen. Some dens are almost townships, with at night a constant coming and going of animals; all the females

1. Den of the lakeside clan, with youngsters

of a clan have their cubs there, and the whole lot of youngsters mixes very amicably. Cubs run around, chasing each other, pestering adults here, rolling in some regurgitated hairballs there, and chewing a bone somewhere else. All ages romp around together, the very small black cubs and the larger spotted ones, for there is no special breeding season. Clearly, the mothers are very much in charge of the outfit; most of the hyaena males stay out of the way of both mothers and cubs.

2, 3, 4. A 6-month old emerges

5. Evening on the den

1. Meeting ceremony between 8-month old cubs

A large, fat mother arrives at nightfall, sniffs another female who is suckling, performs a meeting ceremony with a large cub, then walks to a hole and pokes her head into it. A soft, groaning sound—nothing happens. She walks to another hole and does the same thing; this time her two small black cubs pop out, whining madly, while their mother walks away, lies down, and lets her young ones select a teat. Hyaenas suckle only their own cubs (usually two) and they continue with this until the young ones are well over a year old. By then the cubs are eating meat as well, of course, although this is never taken to them—they have to follow on the hunts and work their way into the scramble after the kill. But the young black cubs just suckle, sometimes for hours on end. I suspect that sometimes they fall asleep there, clutching their teat! Then suddenly the mother has had enough of it, gets up, shakes, and walks off, to start on the night's business—alone, or with a pack of others. The cubs romp around with their playmates a bit longer, then they disappear underground, down the holes which often they have dug themselves and where no adult can follow.

2. Looking for trouble

3. 4 (back to camera) and 6-month old

70

4, 5, 6. Mother arrives, and suckling begins

8-month old cubs whining, begging to suckle

8. The usual suckling posture

71

1. General activity on a den: mothers and offspring, one meeting ceremony

2. Getting to know the other adults

The den is a protection for cubs against lions or against some playful wildebeest or rhino that might chase the little ones. But probably more important is the protection the den affords against other hyaenas, because these animals are straightforward cannibals. If strangers get a chance they will kill and eat the youngsters: when he was six months old our own, tame hyaena Solomon once almost fell victim to an adult intruder and was badly injured, and the photographs show the kind of fate which awaits the cub unprotected by mother and unable to reach the safety of the den to escape an intruder. It is probably just for cub protection, too, that males are kept from the den—although the few which are allowed near spent a great deal of their time there playing with the cubs, performing meeting ceremonies, and hanging around the suckling families.

3. Strange male carrying off his lifeless booty (1-month old cub)

4. Cannibals!

5. Adult hyaenas playing in a pool

6. Play fighting adults

Play

The usual photograph of a hyaena shows a worried-looking animal, with all the cares of the world on its back. But when hyaenas are not interfered with or about to be chased by lions or people, they show an amazing exuberance; they love to play, and even the aged may throw themselves into a boisterous game. And nothing better than playing with water!

Communication

We have come to think of hyaenas as highly gregarious creatures, but that is too simple a description. Communal defence, breeding, hunting—yes, but also for every individual the opportunity to be on its own at least some of the time. Social flexibility is a most important characteristic of hyaena society, a characteristic which allows the species to exploit many different resources efficiently.

Clearly, such a social organization makes very high demands on the species' behavioural repertoire, on the hyaenas' communication. For one individual, every other is a potential killer, but at the same time also a potential collaborator; it is therefore most important for a hyaena to be able to signal to others its moods and intentions. To this end the spotted hyaena has an enormous array of calls, displays, and smells at its disposal—and one has only to see (and hear!) a party on a kill to be convinced of this. The hyaena's melancholy 'whoo-oop' (from low- to high-pitched) is its long-distance call, familiar to anyone who has ever set foot in the African bush (in hyaena language it means just 'I am here'). Aggression is indicated in many different ways—by long moans, deep staccato grunts, or lowing. A fleeing hyaena giggles and yells, or, when actually bitten, growls deeply. All these calls are extremely loud, accompanied by various facial expressions, ear and tail postures, and different attitudes—leaving as little doubt as possible that a message is being driven home to its fellows. So there may be a massive volume of noise on a kill, but there is remarkably little actual fighting—which is a good thing too, in view of the hyaenas' capacity for destruction.

1. Aggressive postures (nearby a lion on their kill): hyaenas left and right lowing loudly, before attack; centre animal yawning, often seen before getting up

2. Flashing teeth in squabble over food

Meeting

Hyaenas perform meeting ceremonies in all sorts of situations, and cubs especially spend a great deal of time going from one meeting ritual to the next. This must be related to what we saw earlier: hyaenas have to be continuously re-integrated with others, because of their partly solitary, partly social existence. When two hyaenas meet, the subdominant ('underdog') usually approaches from downwind, checking up on the other; then, after a cursory sniff at each others' face, the two simultaneously sniff the other's genitals, both lifting a leg (subdominant first). The genitals are now fully erected, whether the animal be a female, a small cub, or an old male: the clitoris can be erected to the same extent as the penis. After a good long sniff the animals go their own way again.

The most striking aspect of the meeting is the display of genitals, and I am sure that the similarity of female and male genitals is related to this ceremony—it has nothing to do with sex by itself. The clitoris looks exactly like a penis and, as well as this, the female also has a sham scrotum, looking very masculine indeed, but with nothing significant inside it. This is the structure which brought into the world the story of hyaenas being hermaphrodites; it goes back to the days of Aristotle, and is still current in Africa today. All tales, of course, but we still don't know enough about it—why this sham penis, or the penis for that matter, is such an important appeasement organ is still a matter of conjecture.

3, 4, 5, 6. Meeting ceremony: approach upwind, first sniff heads, then genitals

1. Mounting: note difference in size

Surprisingly, with the female genitalia being what they are, there is nothing unusual in the hyaenas' copulation. The clitoris shows no signs of erection during sexual behaviour, and the male mounts the female for a relatively short copulation in the usual way. Yet, their mating looks somewhat strange; the male is so much smaller than the female. The male always seems to be cringing around the female; there is no display of strong masculine character here! And if the female does not co-operate there is little else the male can do but paw the ground, looking frustrated—or, as I once saw, rape a cub glaring all the while at the female of his choice.

2. Mounting attempt with uncooperative female. Note the typical chin-on-shoulder posture

Dominance

The hyaena clans are large, and the partly gregarious, partly solitary existence of hyaenas complicates their organization. Understandably, there is no simple dominance rating within a clan, but there are some general rules which seem to apply. For instance, a small animal gives way to a larger one, and cubs follow adults. But one of the most important rules is that females are dominant over males. If the sexes meet, males step aside; if a male is lying in a nice mudhole, he'll make way for the female who wants it. Hunting packs consist of only one or two females and many males—the matriarchs take initiative, others follow.

Obviously, hyaena society has not seen male liberation yet, as we know it from other mammals. But why *should* the male be larger? After all, both sexes defend the territory together, both hunt—only females have to look after the offspring, and keep the possibly cannibalistic males away from their cubs. Clearly, amongst hyaenas there is no premium for the male sex to be larger.

3. Female leads the pack

4. Dominance: two females, one male; the left hand female leads

5. Female takes initiative

Relatives: other Hyaenidae

After having seen something of the complicated life of the spotted hyaena it may be interesting now to have a brief look at its close relatives, just to see the background from which our animal has come. There are only three more members of the family: the striped hyaena, the brown hyaena, and the aardwolf. The first two are real arid-country inhabitants: the striped hyaena in Asia and North and East Africa, the brown hyaena in Southern Africa. The striped one is the classic, scavenging, hyaena type, existing on man's offal around settlements and on pieces of dried bone, but also eating fruits, insects, and reptiles (e.g. tortoises)—things which a spotted hyaena would never touch. The striped hyaena goes through the world alone, through dry bushland and rocky deserts; it occupies large territories, but silently, and only occasionally

does one hear it, softly, when young beg or adults quarrel. Whenever spotted and striped hyaenas meet, as occasionally happens in the Serengeti, stripes give way to spots.

The brown hyaena is at present being studied by Gus Mills in South Africa. This species is even better adapted to desert existence, with an even longer coat and larger feet, covering enormous distances at night in search of fruits, carrion, and small mammal prey. Despite small differences it is essentially like the striped hyaena in its behaviour and ecology —a solitary animal.

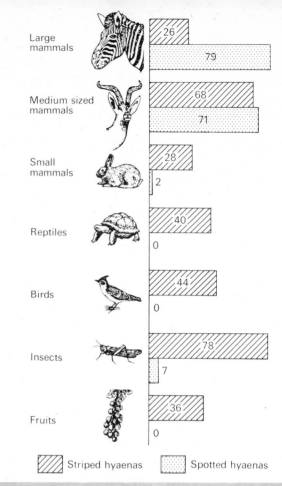

1. Diet of striped and spotted hyaenas in one area of the Serengeti. Figures indicate the percentage of hyaena faeces containing the various categories

Large mammals — Striped 26, Spotted 79
Medium sized mammals — Striped 68, Spotted 71
Small mammals — Striped 28, Spotted 2
Reptiles — Striped 40, Spotted 0
Birds — Striped 44, Spotted 0
Insects — Striped 78, Spotted 7
Fruits — Striped 36, Spotted 0

▨ Striped hyaenas   ▦ Spotted hyaenas

78

2. Striped hyaena in dry Commiphera woodland, Serengeti

3. Typical striped hyaena habitat in Israel